...And Daddy Will Always Love You

First Edition

Author: Kyle Walkine

ISBN-13: 978-0-9995456-2-1

Cover Art: Mecko Gibson
Illustrations: Mecko Gibson
IG: MeckoGibsonArt

Published: Kyle Walkine, Mecko Gibson

FOREWORD

"And Daddy Will Always Love You" was written to serve as a letter from fathers to their children.

It was written by the author Kyle Walkine, just a few days after the birth of his son Kaylen.

A journalist himself, Kyle sought to find a way to immortalize his love for his son. But taking it beyond himself, Kyle wanted to write the book so other fathers would be able to read to their children as a bedtime story.

Kyle wrote *"And Daddy Will Always Love You"* with this in mind: It's a letter for fathers to tell their children no matter where they go or decisions they make, they can always look over their shoulder and see their father supporting them.

No matter where they go, what they decide to do, Daddy will always love them.

– KYLE WALKINE

- For all fathers and their children.

You'll be the best at whatever you do.

One day you'll grow up to be a doctor,
teacher, or whatever it is you want.

But wherever you go, you know this will always be true;

I will always be there and daddy will always love you.

Soon it'll be time for school.

You'll learn and play with your friends and have a new adventure every day.

Late at night when you are fast asleep,
you're still on daddy's mind.

And as you open your big bright eyes
to see the skies of blue...

One thing is for certain:
daddy will always love you.

CPSIA information can be obtained
at www.ICGtesting.com
Printed in the USA
LVHW070757190621
690646LV00005B/42